SUPER CITIES!

CHICAGO

by Mark Shulman

arcadia®
CHILDREN'S BOOKS

Published by Arcadia Children's Books
A Division of Arcadia Publishing
Charleston, SC
www.arcadiapublishing.com

Super Cities is a trademark of Arcadia Publishing, Inc.

First published 2021

ISBN 978-1-5402-5065-0

Library of Congress Control Number: 2021943261

Notice: The information in this book is true and complete to the best of our knowledge. It is off ered without guarantee on the part of the author or Arcadia Publishing. The author and Arcadia Publishing disclaim all liability in connection with the use of this book.

Produced by Shoreline Publishing Group LLC
Santa Barbara, California
Designer: Patty Kelley

Contents

Chicago!

Is Chicago your kind of town?

When Chicago became a city in 1837, it sat at the wild western frontier of the United States. Nearly 200 years later, it's right in the center. And it's the largest city between New York City and Los Angeles!

Chicago is famous for many reasons. It once had the world's tallest building and the tallest *T. rex* skeleton. It still has the world's largest food festival, and the thickest pizza. It's even got the largest, shiniest metal vegetable in the known

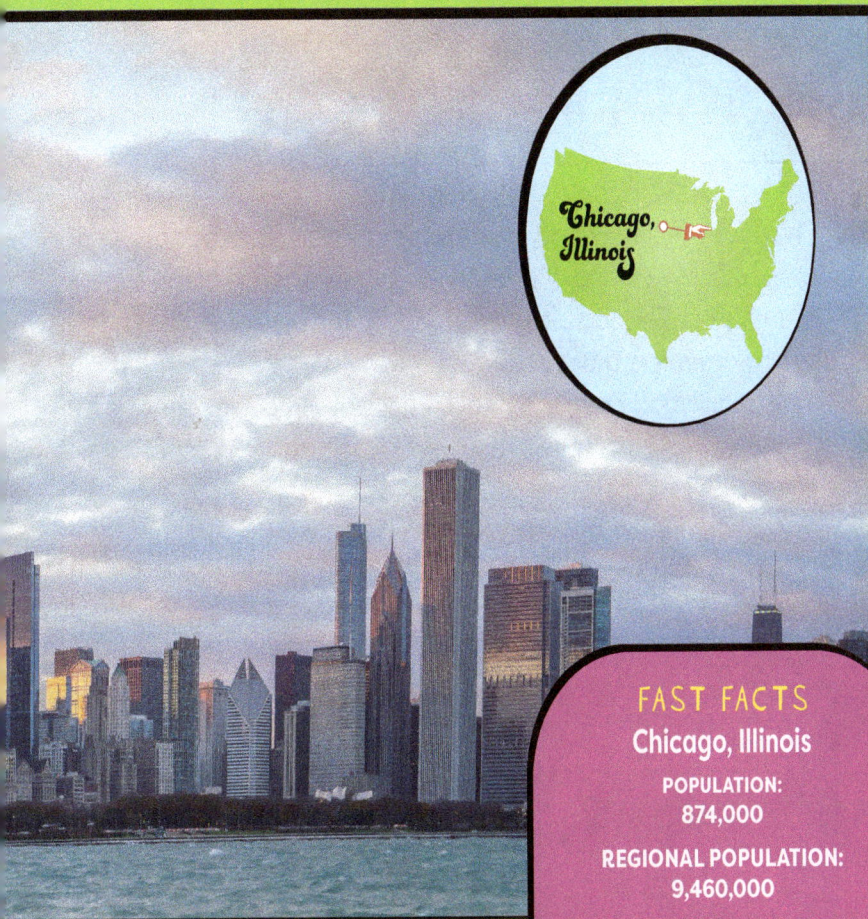

universe! Keep reading—you'll find out about all this, and more!

When you're in Chicago, you'll see how the entire city spreads along the Lake Michigan shoreline. The local kids have long, beautiful beaches to play on, right in the middle of the city!

If you arrive by water, you won't be alone. Chicago's seaport is the world's largest and busiest inland (not-on-an-ocean) port! And if you arrive by water, you'll see why Chicago was the world's first skyscraper city! Let's head to Chicago!

CHICAGO: Map It!

Chicago is the largest city in the state of Illinois. The city sits on the southwestern end of Lake Michigan, which is one of the five Great Lakes. Chicago is a growing city, to the north, west, and south—anywhere that's dry!

So many roads lead to Chicago. Highways sprout in every direction. And before the highways, Chicago was the central hub of the 19th century U.S. railroad empire.

Don't forget the ships! They come from across the Atlantic Ocean, to the Great Lakes, and the final stop is Chicago!

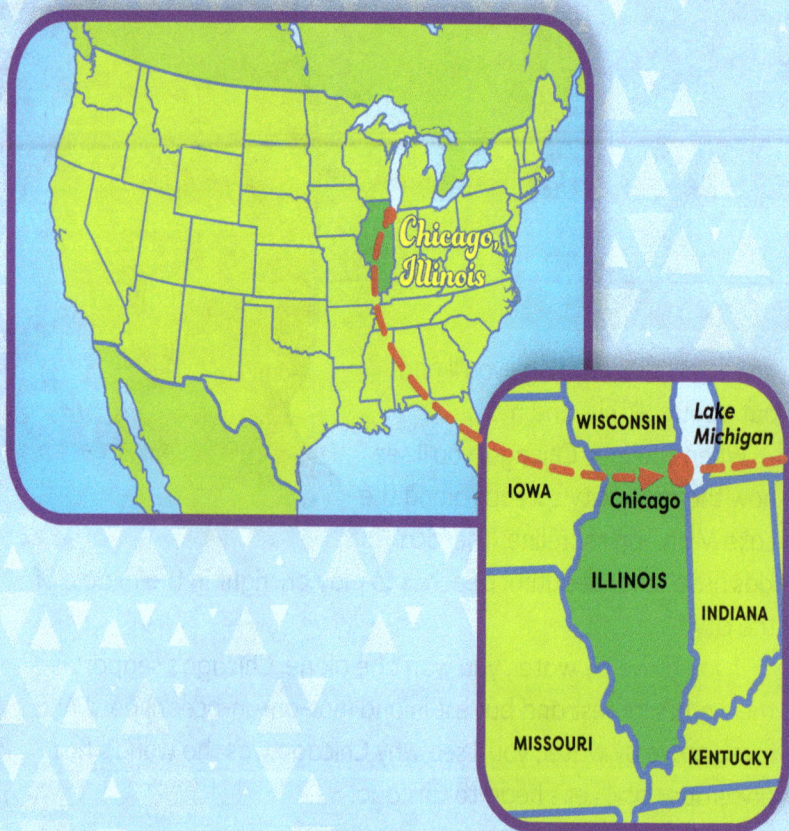

Chicago, Illinois

WISCONSIN
Lake Michigan
IOWA
Chicago
ILLINOIS
INDIANA
MISSOURI
KENTUCKY

N

Lake Michigan

O'Hare
International
Airport

Lincoln
Park

Navy Pier

Millennium Park/The Bean

The Loop

Northerly Island

Chicago River

KEY

City limits

Parks

State border

Outdoors!

In a big, busy city, you want a place to step back into nature and enjoy some green. Chicago comes through!

The city has a system of eight connected parks that stretches 26 miles from north to south., These parks run along the shoreline. They are criss-crossed with an impressive collection of beautiful roads, bike trails, hiking trails, mansions, and famous museums.

Northerly Island, on Chicago's South Side, is a green oasis jutting into Lake Michigan, with walking paths, fishing, and the greatest city views.

Twice as big as New York's Central Park, the 1,700-acre Morton Arboretum has 16 miles of trails and more than 200,000 plants to walk along. Best of all, there's also a huge children's garden and a real maze garden to get lost in!

If you like beautiful outdoor spaces surrounded by great buildings, you'll love your time in Chicago!

CHICAGO MEANS . . .

When it comes to city names, Chicago stinks. Literally!

Long before white settlers came, the Native Algonquian people called the area *shikaakwa*. And what did that mean? "Stinky onion." This lovely name was fine, but slightly off, since the forests were actually loaded with stinky garlic, not onion. Early French settlers who arrived in the late 1600s heard the name and wrote it down as *Chicagou*.

That's the official story. But there are others. Some believe *Chicagoua* was a Native word for "skunk," which is a pretty similar idea. *Shecaugo* translated to "playful waters." And then there was Chief Chi-ca-gua, of the nearby Mitchigamea people, whose name meant "he who stands by the tree." Take your pick!

The Bowman is one of two huge statues in Grant Park. The other is the Spearman.

What about Illinois? "The Illinois" was the name of a confederation of Native nations in the region.

This is the form of wild garlic that gave Chicago its name!

PIER PLEASURE!

Where can kids in Chicago have the most fun in the least amount of space? Navy Pier, right in the center of the city!

Since 1916, the 3,300-foot pier has been a dock for ships, a jail, a college, a theater, and a World War II Navy training center where nearly 10,000 people lived and worked. Since 1995, it has been home to tons of fun!

Light Tower, a vertical drop ride!

Funhouse Maze, a vast labyrinth of tunnels and mazes!

Remote Control Boats, with your own yachts to navigate!

Festivals, parties, competitions, and concerts. Plus . . . Fireworks, over and over again!

Centennial Wheel, a 200-foot Ferris wheel with 41 gondolas!

Wave Swinger, a fast-spinning, sky-high carousel ride!

Children's Museum, with all you'd expect!

Crystal Gardens, a six-story glass botanical garden!

Shakespeare and IMAX theaters, for even more fun!

The Algonquian tribes who settled near Lake Michigan were called the Illinois Nation. They were made up of many smaller nations. Closest to modern Chicago was the Council of the Three Fires: the Ojibwe, Odawa, and Potawatomi Nations. Every nation was made up of smaller clans. Young people could only marry someone from a different clan. This helped create tribal unity.

These Nations had a thriving culture. Women held positions of leadership, and sometimes joined the hunt. Different families lived together in longhouses and wigwams.

Lacrosse, a team sport created in the Algonquian Nation, is still played today. It began as a serious form of battle training. Teams were split according to odd and even birth order.

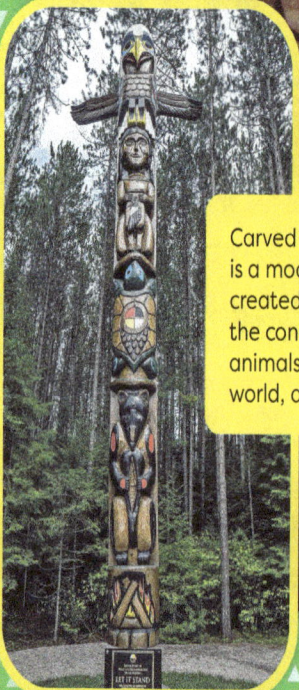

Carved wooden poles (this is a modern version) were created to symbolize the connection between animals and the natural world, and people.

The Illinois were skilled in arts and crafts, weaving, and stonework. Dolls were detailed with beads, leather, and cloth. Wampum beads were exchanged like money.

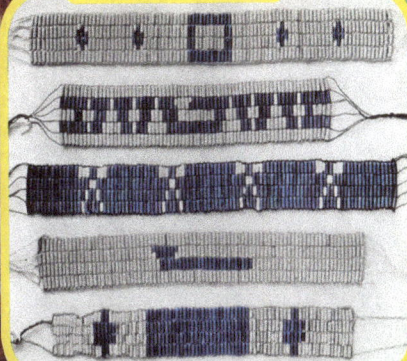

HISTORY: It's a City!

1673: Two French explorers, Marquette and Joliet, send the first news of the Chicago area back to Europe.

1780s: Jean Baptiste Point du Sable, a free Black man, becomes the first settler of Chicago, which was then home only to Native peoples. He's recognized today as the founder of Chicago. In du Sable's time, most Black people in America were enslaved, so this is a big deal!

1803: The U.S. Army erects Fort Dearborn, along the Chicago River. The wooden stockade stood at what is now the corner of Michigan Avenue and Wacker Drive. Ten years later, the Pottawatomi burn the fort during the War of 1812.

Jean-Baptiste Pointe DuSable
1745-1818
Founder of Chicago

August 12, 1833: Just twelve years after the Illinois territory became the 21st state, the Town of Chicago was established. The sleepy frontier town had just 350 residents. It is about half the size of what is now the downtown "Loop" area. Fields and farms surround the town itself.

1848: The Illinois and Michigan Canal opens, connecting Lake Michigan— and the rest of the Great Lakes—to the mighty Mississippi River. Ships coming from Buffalo, New York, can now reach the Gulf of Mexico directly. Chicago business booms.

1860: Railroads, the newest technology, are crossing the country from coast to coast. At least 30 pass through Chicago. This fast-growing city has become the nation's transportation center. Factories and warehouses quickly replace fields and farms. By 1870, Chicago will soon become the nation's fifth-largest city with 300,000 residents.

HISTORY: The Fire and the Fair

October 8-10, 1871: Tragedy! It's the Great Chicago Fire! One-third of the quickly growing city is destroyed and left in ashes.

What happened? It had been a long, hot summer and fall without rain. On the evening of October 8, a fire began near a barn in southwestern Chicago. The blaze rapidly spread through neighborhoods packed tight with wooden buildings. High winds carried the flames across the Chicago River to the North Side. Firefighters were not able to control the fire, which burned for two days.

FAST FACT

Legend says Mrs. O'Leary's cow kicked over a lantern, which started the fire. Except that's just a legend. Nobody knows how the fire really started.

This water tower on Michigan Avenue is one of the few buildings to survive the fire.

1880s: The Great Fire didn't keep Chicago down for long! The city was rebuilt very quickly. Within 20 years, hundreds of new buildings replaced the lost ones. And best of all, new rules were created to make buildings safer and more fireproof. Chicago was bigger and better than ever!

1893: The World's Columbian Exposition opened. Nearly 700 acres of structures, canals, roadways, fountains, and more, were built in Jackson Park. Nearly 200 buildings, all white, all temporary, were built very quickly. People were astonished by a new invention called "light bulbs," which changed the night forever. They named this marvelous place the White City, and with good reason!

From May 1 to October 30, 1893, more than 27 million people visited the exposition, or expo. That's about 150,000 each day. They came to see the architecture and exhibits from 46 countries. Many lined up for a ride invented by George Washington Gale Ferris, Jr. Yes, the Ferris Wheel was invented for Chicago's World's Fair! At 264 feet tall, 2,160 people could ride at the same time. There was nothing like it.

FAST FACT

Why Columbian? 1893 was the 400th anniversary of the first arrival of Christopher Columbus, in 1492. Well, actually the 401st!

HISTORY: Chicago Grows Up

1885: The Home Insurance Building becomes the world's first skyscraper. With its iron and steel skeleton stretching 10 stories into the sky, it stood a whopping 138 feet (42 meters) tall. Six years later, another two floors were added. All 12 floors were demolished in 1931 to make way for more and bigger buildings.

June 6, 1892: Chicago's elevated ("El") train line began service. Soon it would become one of the country's three busiest transit systems, and grow to eight lines and 102 miles of track.

1919: The World Series this season was a sad one for Chicago. It turned out that several Chicago White Sox players had lost on purpose to help gamblers win big. The players were caught and those White Sox were called the Black Sox!

1920s: The "Roaring Twenties" were Chicago's gangster years. They began soon after Prohibition laws made alcohol illegal. Crime bosses like Al Capone and "Bugs" Moran fought to control the city's organized crime. Things calmed down by the 1930s.

1940s: Chicago helps the U.S. gear up for World War II. The city becomes the nation's second-largest war goods manufacturer, after Detroit. Airplanes, engines, torpedoes, and even parachutes were stamped Made in Chicago! Thanks to the newly available jobs, tens of thousands of Black Americans from the South headed to Chicago and other northern cities in what was called the Great Migration (see page 22).

1959: The Saint Lawrence Seaway officially opens. Now ships can get from the Atlantic Ocean, through Canada, to the Great Lakes and Chicago. And back again!

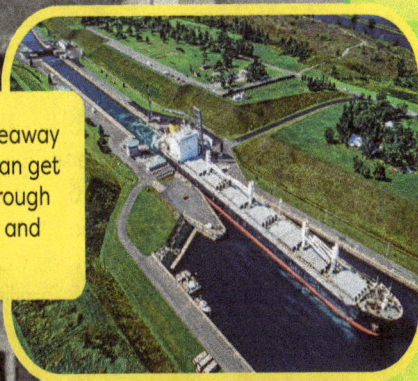

1968: Though the Democratic Convention (held to choose a person to run for president for that party) led to riots in Chicago streets, the movement for social change was inspired by the young people who protested.

1974: The 108-story Sears (now Willis) Tower becomes the world's tallest building.

Black History in Chicago

The African American community in Chicago has had a long and rich impact on the culture and history of the city. The first non-Indigenous person to settle there was Jean Baptiste du Sable in 1778, a Black man from Haiti. He lived among the Indigenous tribes in the area and created a highly successful trade route that began the city of Chicago!

In 1916 the Great Migration began. From then until 1970 more than six million African Americans moved from the rural South to northern cities, including Chicago. (*Migration* means "the movement of people from one place to another.") The main reason for this migration was to escape terrible poverty and racist laws and people in the South. African Americans were looking for better jobs with better pay. They wanted to build homes and raise their families in the North. The *Chicago Defender* newspaper was written and published by the African American community. It featured stories of success and printed ads for jobs and homes that encouraged people to make the move.

While Black Chicagoans were able to find some of what they were looking for in the city, they still faced racist laws, policies, and people. The laws said where Black people could (and

Housing laws sometimes forced Black families into small apartments (above). Later, World War II created many new opportunities for work, especially for women.

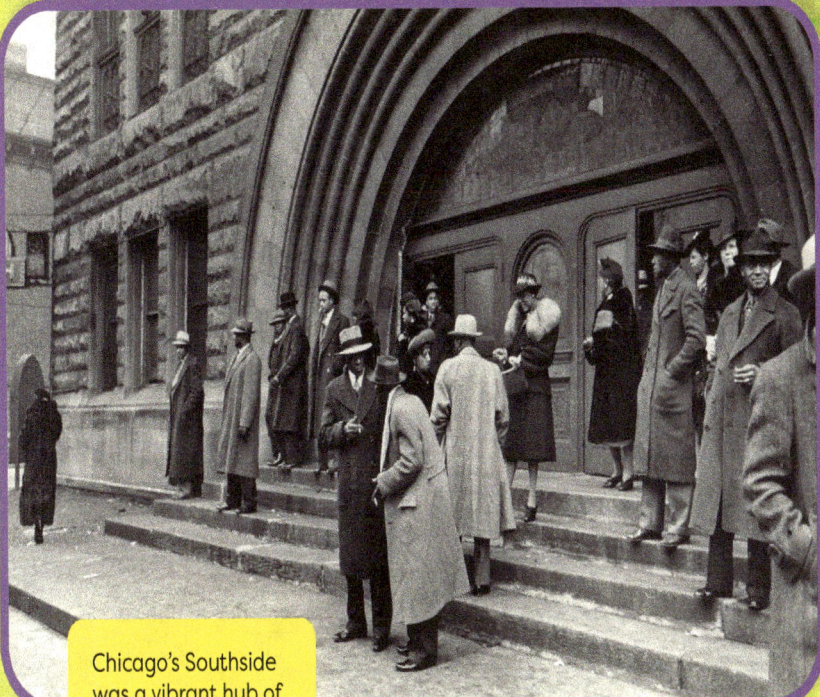

Chicago's Southside was a vibrant hub of Black life and culture.

could not) live and spend their free time. The Civil Rights movement began there in 1919 following the Chicago race riot and the refusal of the police to arrest a white man who had murdered a Black child. For more than 100 years, very important African American leaders, citizens, and veterans of the armed services have been protesting against injustice and fighting for equal rights. In 1983, Harold Washington became Chicago's first Black mayor. President Barack Obama built his career as a lawyer and community organizer in Chicago.

Today the neighborhoods of Bronzeville and Hyde Park are major hubs of Black culture and history. You can find museums, galleries, historic homes, and monuments there. African Americans also brought jazz and blues music to Chicago, which is a major part of its culture today. Chicago was home to famous Black people like architect Walter T. Bailey, pilot and stunt flier Bessie Coleman, journalist and activist Ida B. Wells, musician Louis Armstrong, astronaut Mae Jemison, and cardiologist Dr. Daniel Hale Williams, who performed the first successful open-heart surgery!

CHICAGO TODAY

Chicago is the nation's third-largest city, after New York and Los Angeles. Here are some of the reasons Chicago stands so tall.

Transportation: Ships, trains, and highways have always converged in Chicago. So do airplanes. O'Hare Airport, which is a hub (main airport) for both United Airlines and American Airlines, is the nation's third busiest airport.

FAST FACT

The Fig Newton was invented in Chicago, made in the world's largest bakery!

Food: A mighty city can get mighty hungry. Chicago's famous deep-dish pizza is so thick, you need a knife and fork. The hot dogs are hefty. The steakhouses serve some of the country's best. And for dessert, there's the rainbow cone: five flavors of sherbet stacked onto a cone.

Music: The city is known for its music festivals. Chicago's blues music has a wide range of African-American sounds that are also the roots of rock music. Famous Chicago blues musicians include Muddy Waters, Howlin' Wolf, Willie Dixon, and Buddy Guy.

Architecture: More than once, Chicago has led the way, creating the tallest, the most elegant, or the most original architecture. They call North Michigan Avenue "The Magnificent Mile" for the remarkable buildings, and the magnificent shopping inside them.

Get Outdoors!: Not even the Windy City's wind and cold can keep Chicagoans from enjoying nature. You'll find kayaks on the Chicago River, paddleboards on Lake Michigan, runners and bikers on Lakefront trails, and rock climbers at Maggie Daley Park. Plus, it's a great walking city!

Is the Windy City Really Windy?

Chicago Climate and Weather

Can you guess why Chicago was first called "The Windy City?" Not for the weather, but because long-ago politicians gave long, windy speeches! Still, like any northern area, Chicago usually has hot summers, chilly winters, and milder weather in between. Here's what's you can really expect from the weather, and why.

It Keeps Changing

Here's an old Chicago joke: "Don't like the weather? Wait a minute!" It's no joke. On cold days, Chicago skies can be clear, then gray, then stormy, then clear again. Why? That's typical of northern climates, especially if there isn't an ocean nearby bringing warm air. Chicagoans know how to prepare for changes in weather.

Flakes, Flurries, and F-F-Freezing!

In winter, a constant flow of cold air, called the polar jet stream, brings rain, sleet, hail, ice storms . . . and snow! From delicate powder to flurries to blinding blizzards, Chicago gets 36 inches of snow each year, and another 36 inches of rain.

Great Effect of the Great Lakes

Lake Michigan has a big influence on Chicago's weather. In summer, the lake brings cool breezes. In winter, when cold northern air passes over less-cold lake water, the now-warmer air turns to moisture. The moisture turns to snow. Sometimes lots of snow. And that's called a "lake effect."

FAST FACT

Actually, Chicago is only the 14th windiest city in the U.S.. Dodge City, Kansas, often earns the top spot.

Building Climate Change

Here's another thing that changes Chicago's weather: the buildings! Those and other big man-made objects—roads, sidewalks, parking lots, and cars—store heat and raise Chicago's temperature a few degrees higher than in nearby rural areas. That's called the "urban heat island effect."

Hey! I Lived in Chicago!

We could fill a book with amazing people from Chicago. Here are some folks you might like to meet.

Barack Obama:
The 44th President was born in Hawaii, but spent many years on Chicago's South Side. In 1992, he began teaching at the University of Chicago Law School. He was elected to the Illinois Senate in 1997, and was elected U.S. Senator from Illinois in 2004. The Obamas still have a home in Kenwood, on Chicago's South Side, not far from where his presidential library will be located in Jackson Park.

John C. Reilly
What do *Guardians of the Galaxy*, *Wreck-It Ralph*, and *Gangs of New York* have in common? They all feature actor and comedian John C. Reilly. Famous for his doughy face and sweet personality, Reilly grew up in the Chicago Lawn neighborhood.

Oprah Winfrey

An actress, a talk-show host, a businessperson, she is one of the most famous people in the world . . . and she got her start on TV in Chicago in 1983. She broadcast most of her shows from the city until 2011.

Michael Jordan

Very few players or teams win their championship trophy three years in a row. Chicago Bulls basketball legend Michael Jordan did it *twice*. He was also named MVP after all six victories! Jordan was drafted by Chicago in 1984, where he played until 1998. In addition to his sneaker empire, Jordan founded a Chicago-area Boys & Girls Club in honor of his father.

The late comedian and actor **Robin Williams** was born just north of Chicago, in the city of Lake Forest. The hyper-energetic funnyman said he was very shy in junior high. From *Mork and Mindy* to his standup comedy specials to many award-winning movie roles, it's hard to believe this imaginative, fast-paced, brilliant mind could ever have been considered shy.

Things to see in Chicago

Chicago-area kids know what an amazing place they live in. If you're new in town, you'll appreciate some of these fun and fascinating things to do. Let's start with an overview of the city. Literally!

Skydeck Chicago

At 108 stories and 1,450 feet tall, Willis Tower (once called Sears Tower) was the world's tallest building from 1974 to 1998. It's still pretty tall. Don't believe it? Step onto the glass-bottomed Skydeck (left). You'll know what it's like to float a quarter-mile off the ground!

TILT at 360 Chicago

There's a different kind of sky-high view at 875 N. Michigan Ave. (previously the John Hancock building). Up high on the 360-degree deck, you'll be able to see all of Chicago, as well as four states, while you're standing 1,000 feet in the air.

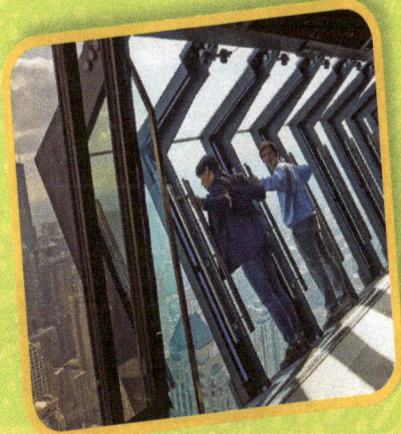

The Bean

Few sculptures are as popular as **Cloud Gate**, which everyone in Chicago calls "**the Bean**." It's big (66 feet long, and 33 feet high) and it's heavy (nearly 110 tons) and best of all, it's shiny! This stainless steel sculpture is a great warped mirror in Millennium Park. Even in winter, you'll see kids of all ages lying under the Bean to catch a funhouse view of themselves!

Millennium Park Beyond the Bean, Millennium Park has world-class attractions. The Crown Fountain features dozens of splashable waterspouts, and two 50-foot glass brick video towers featuring faces that actually soak you with water! Dry off among Lurie Garden's wildflowers . . . the weird, warped Boeing sculpture galleries . . . or watch a show on the lawn at the sprawling, futuristic Jay Pritzker Pavilion. In winter there's an ice rink.

Maggie Daley Park

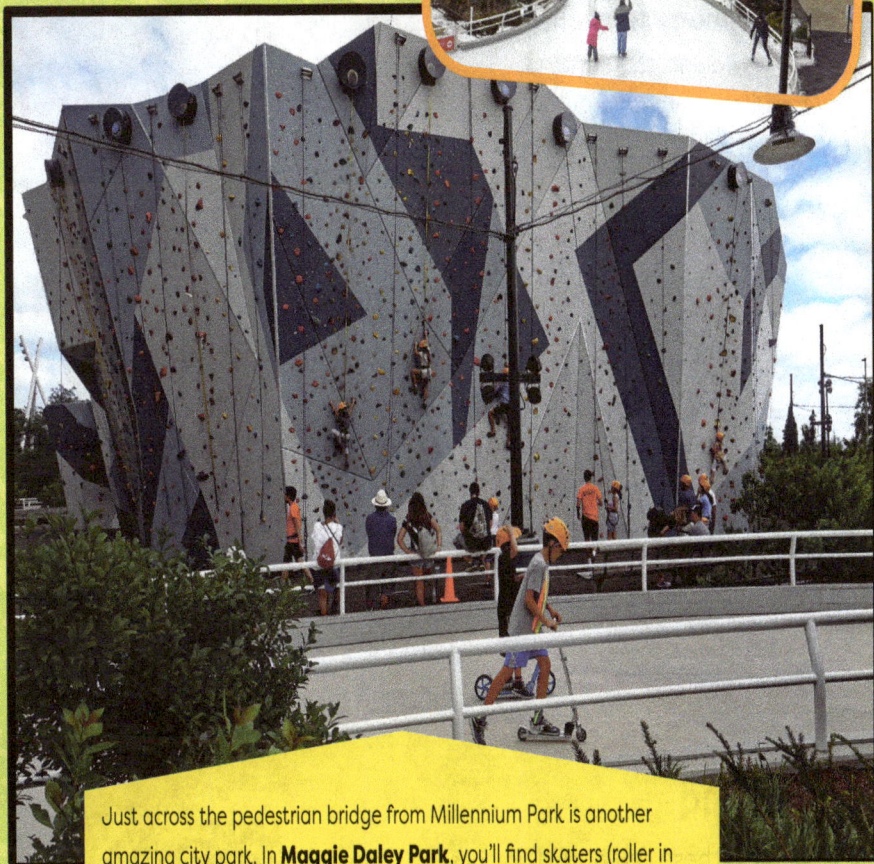

Just across the pedestrian bridge from Millennium Park is another amazing city park. In **Maggie Daley Park**, you'll find skaters (roller in summer, ice in winter) taking long loops on the quarter-mile Skating Ribbon. Inside there's a vast Play Garden that's part sculpture garden, part fairy tale forest, and 100% unique playground. There are slides, climbers, and a miniature golf course with its own miniature Willis Tower!

Wait, there's *more*? The central feature at Maggie Daley Park is hard to miss. Conquer the two 40-foot rock climbing walls of sculptured steel along the edge of the lake. Up to 100 folks can climb the slanted slopes at the same time. And best of all, kids can play in this park for *free*!

Beaches!

Chicago may be 800 miles from the nearest ocean, but its beach scene is hopping. And it's convenient! There are 26 miles of human-made beaches on the length of the city's lakeshore. Bring your sunscreen and swimsuits . . . wherever you see a lifeguard, it's safe to jump in!

Burnham Skate Park

These vast concrete bowls look like moon craters, except for the rails, the grind box, the ramps, and the quarter pipe. Whether your wheels fit a skateboard, rollerblade, scooter, or BMX, you'll find plenty to challenge you at this pro-level park on the waterfront. Find more free, city-run skateparks at Wilson Park, Grant Park, and Logan Blvd.

Legoland

If you love these brick building toys, you'll love Legoland Discovery Center. You can build and race Lego cars, see a complete version of Chicago in bricks, and go on Lego-themed rides. Bring your creativity!

Shedd Aquarium

Do you want to visit a coral reef, watch dolphins play, and experience a piranha feeding frenzy? Want to learn more about conserving our oceans? If you said yes, your aquatic journey can stay in Chicago. Since 1929, the majestic Shedd Aquarium has been bringing a world of undersea wonders (with underwater views!) to the landlubbers of Chicagoland. You can touch stingrays, visit a reef, and watch dolphins and otters play (though not together!).

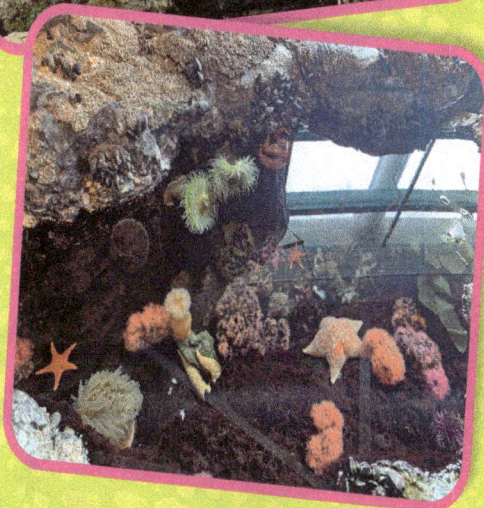

Tall Ship *Windy*

This four-masted sailing ship takes its name—and its way of getting around—from the city's nickname. Since 2008, it has been taking visitors and school groups around Lake Michigan to experience what life was like on old-time sailing ships. If you go, get ready to work: On some trips, passengers help pull the ropes to raise the sails!

GETTING AROUND

CHICAGO

A city of nearly three million people (plus six million neighbors in the region) needs many ways to get around. Chicago has the usual buses, taxis, ride shares, and suburban commuter trains. But there are a boatload of other options.

Share and Share a Bike
Want to pedal but don't want to park it? Try Divvy, the city's bike share program. For a reasonable fee, locals can borrow any of the 6,000 turquoise bikes, get exercise, save the planet, then drop it off, worry-free, at nearly 600 different stations.

From Underground to Overhead

Chicago loves its train system. It has plenty of tunnels, but you can't call it a subway. They call it the "El," short for "elevated railroad." That's because these trains spend much of the time at street level, or up on tracks high off the ground. It's loud, it's convenient, and it rolls by third-floor windows, 24 hours a day.

Water Taxis Ahoy!

They're called taxis, but they travel the city like floating buses. Water taxis travel to several key points in the city, along the Chicago River. These boats also connect to bus and train lines. If the weather's good enough, float to your destination in style!

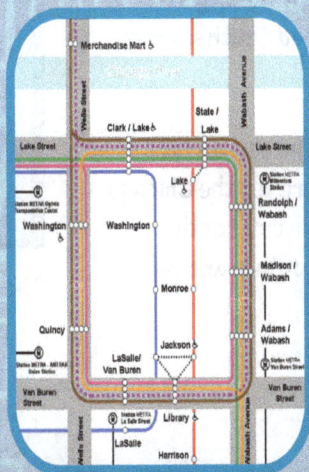

Loop the Loop

Just as all roads lead to Rome, all eight CTA train lines lead downtown. Together, they make eight stops on a 1.8 mile loop around many of Chicago's most important business and government buildings. You can switch from one train line to another, or you can go around and around and around and . . .

IT'S OFFICIAL!

Every city and state seems to have a bunch of "official" stuff that's so important, or so locally loved, their government makes an "official" declaration and tells everybody, "Pay attention!" Here's what's "official" in Chicago!

OFFICIAL CITY SYMBOL:
The Y symbol, also called the Municipal Device, is meant to represent the Chicago River and its North and South branches.

OFFICIAL CITY FLAG:

The top and bottom white stripes are for the city's North and South sides.

The blue stripes are for the Chicago River's north and south branches.

The red stars are for 4 major Chicago events:

* Fort Dearborn, the first white settlement (1803)
* The Great Chicago Fire (1871)
* The World Columbian Exposition (1893)
* The Century of Progress Exposition (1933)

The first flag, from 1917, had only two stars. The next two stars were added in 1933 and 1939.

OFFICIAL CITY FLOWER:
Chrysanthemum

OFFICIAL CITY MOTTO:
"Urbs in Horto,"
which is Latin for
"City in a garden."

OFFICIAL STUFF OF ILLINOIS

Bird:
Northern cardinal

Flower:
Violet

Fish:
Bluegill

Vegetable:
Sweet corn

Animal:
White-tailed Deer

For some reason, people call the 50-foot Pablo Picasso sculpture in Richard Daley plaza "**the Picasso Sculpture**." Actually, it's untitled.

Art in Chicago

Ask a Chicago native to name their favorite work of public art, they might say the Bean. Or they might say the deep-dish pizza. Beyond that, the city has world-class art that isn't even about food!

Outdoor Art

Chicago is a big art city. And when it comes to outdoor sculpture, we mean *big*.

Outside the amazing Adler Planetarium, Henry Moore's **Man Enters the Cosmos** looks like it should hold a missing globe. It's just 13 feet tall, but it's still too big for your bedroom.

Alexander Calder's 53-foot **Flamingo** perches in Chicago's Federal Plaza, ready to swoop down on the area's government workers.

Legs on parade! **Agora**, by Magdalena Abakanowicz, features 106 headless lower bodies. Each is 9 feet tall, 1,800 pounds, and "walks" aimlessly around Grant Park while you walk aimlessly between them.

Great Museums!

Chicago is a museum city. And you've got choices: big, small, famous, quirky, specialized, or some combo of the above. There's no shortage of interesting, informative, interactive excitement for kids of every age to love!

The Art Institute of Chicago: Two lions protect the impressive, vast stone entrance of the Midwest's largest art museum. They need to be on guard, considering all the famous paintings, sculptures, and more, so much more, waiting for you inside. The museum is especially well-known for its American and European arts, African and Native arts, Asian arts, Arms & Armor and ... wait for it ... a collection of 1,400 paperweights!

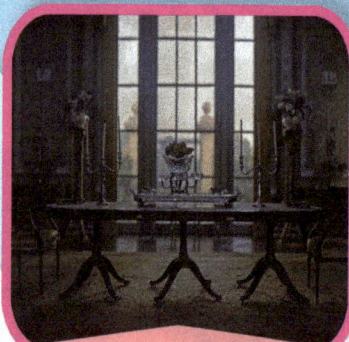

The **Thorne Miniature Rooms** are 68 unique, super-detailed, small-scale rooms, including historic reproductions of famous interiors!

Younger kids can't get enough of the **Chicago Children's Museum** on Navy Pier. They'll joyfully explore the interactive worlds of dinosaurs, waterways, treehouse trails, and more. Kids can climb, crawl, feel, listen . . . anything but eat the exhibits.

The Bronzeville Children's Museum was the first African American children's museum when it opened in 1993. Visitors can find out about Black inventors, see how Chicago has been changed by African Americans, and explore lots of hands-on adventures!

Other Great Chicago Museums

The Field Museum: You know you're in the right place when a giant *T. rex* bares its teeth at the entrance. The Field doesn't just show exhibits—they make each display feel like a real world. Visit Cleopatra's ancient Egypt . . . see things from a bug's perspective in the Underground Adventure . . . take a nature walk through different habitats . . . and feel the intensity of slavery-era Africa. As a finale, see the best-lit jades and gems anywhere.

Meet Sue! Visitors to the Field are always excited to see Sue, one of the largest and most complete *T. rex* skeletons in the world. The fossil was discovered by Sue Hendrickson in 1990 in South Dakota. Sue (the dinosaur) lived more than 67 million years ago. Sue (the skeleton) has taught millions of people all about how dinos looked and lived.

The Museum of Science and Industry: What's in the Palace of Fine Arts, the last remaining 1893 Exposition building? An awesome science museum! The interactive displays are world class, and they keep creating new ones. Tour a coal mine, walk through a human heart, see robot toymakers in action, marvel at a lunar module, board a real U-boat and a luxury train from the 1930s. And the building? Magnificent!

DuSable Museum of African American History: Since 1961, this is the nation's oldest independent museum that studies culture, history, artwork and artifacts of African and African-American people. It's named for the founder of Chicago (page 16). Kids will find special exhibits and events just for them, along with movies, concerts, and presentations.

Chicago History Museum: The city celebrates itself in this interactive history experience. Want to visit an old Chicago street? Or ride on the first "El" train? You can explore the sounds and smells of the Great Chicago Fire, an old jazz club, a stock yard, a baseball park. And if you feel hungry, turn yourself into a Chicago hot dog!

Robie House: A house? We're going to a house? Frank Lloyd Wright is considered one of the most brilliant architects of the 20th century, and this house is considered one of his masterpieces. Once you see Wright's signature "prairie style" on the outside and the interiors with perfectly designed furniture, you'll see why this house is so different than any other. Wright lived in nearby Oak Park; visitors can find many examples of his work in Chicagoland.

Performing Arts

What kind of music do you like best? Chances are, on any day, some amazing musician is performing it in Chicago. The region has hundreds of concert halls, theaters, clubs, restaurants, and smaller venues, inside and out. There are way too many to name. That's why they invented the internet!

Okay, we'll name one. The Jay Pritzker Pavilion is a wild-looking, bandshell in the middle of Millennium Park. Looping metal surrounds the stage, like a giant steel apple that got peeled. Crazy? Not to your ears. More than 11,000 people can gather in the seats and on the lawn to see and hear all kinds of performances, from alternative and classical to yoga and zydeco.

Festivals!

Chicago is well-known for an astonishing number of music festivals each year. The fences go up, the speakers roll in, the lights come on, the bands come out. Audiences flock from around the world, packing Chicago's theaters and lawns to soak up its festivals.

Annual Performing Arts Events

These festivals run from late spring to early fall each year. And there are more! Check the local listings for dates, times, and places.

Type of Music	Festival
Alternative	Pitchfork Music Festival
Alternative	Lollapalooza
Blues	Chicago Blues Festival
Caribbean	Chicago Carifete
Classical	Grant Park Music Festival
Country	Chicago Country Music Festival
Gospel	Chicago Gospel Festival
Hip-Hop	Summer Smash Festival
Latin	Ruido Fest
Jazz	Chicago Jazz Festival
Local	Chicago In Tune
Rock	Rock Around the Block

How to Talk Chicago

Chicagoans have their own way of talking, with their own special words. Spend any time in the Windy City and you're sure to hear some of these.

"I'm Gonna Dip"

That means you've decided to go.

Prairie

A vacant lot, usually in a neighborhood.

GYM SHOES

sneakers. Just . . . regular sneakers. Even if they've never been to a gym.

The EL

The EL-evated train, described using the fewest syllables possible.

Frunchroom

That's the front room in a house. Chicago words often get smashed together.

Grachki

The garage key. More smashed together words.

CHICAGO: It's Weird!

Green For a Day

Chicago has the luck of a lot of Irish residents. Every March 17, St. Patrick's Day is a big event. The Chicago River gets a one-day, emerald green makeover while the city celebrates.

The Puppet Bike

An artist named Jason Trusty attached a working puppet show theater to . . . you guessed it . . . a bike. He performs a puppet show that can be even weirder.

Oz Park

How much do you love *The Wizard of Oz*? Would you make a theme park? Or, rather, a park with a theme? Because someone did. It's filled with statues and tributes to Dorothy, Toto, the Wicked Witch, and other characters from the 1939 film.

The American Toby Jug Museum

What's a Toby Jug? It's a large, ceramic mug in the shape of somebody's head. Somebody with a hat, plus other details. You're supposed to drink from it. Better to start a museum and shelve it there instead.

The Antique Fabricare Museum

If you were going to dedicate a museum to old-fashioned laundry tools, like ancient irons and clunky steamers and long-forgotten soap brands, wouldn't you put it in a dry cleaning place? Of course you would.

Chicago 51

CHICAGO for Everyone

Chicago is a city of intensity and diversity. What's the best way to discover the international flavor (and flavors) of a city? Explore the many neighborhoods that different ethnic groups and cultures call home.

FAST FACT

Every July, Grant Park hosts the world's largest food festival. For five days, you can eat around the world and barely move.

Greek Chicago: Greektown

The Greek culture is one of the world's oldest, and you'll find history in every Greek restaurant, taverna, bakery and café in Greektown. No matter how good the food (and music) may be, you have to save room for the incredible desserts. Tell your grown-ups we said so. Landmark: the National Hellenic Museum. Event: The annual Greek Independence Day Parade in spring.

People from China

When you see the dragons, the Chinese lettering, and the giant arched gateway, you'll know you've arrived. For more than 100 years, Chinatown has been bringing Chicago the sights, smells, and tastes of Chinese culture. Landmark: The Chinese American Museum of Chicago or the Nine Dragon Wall.

Indian Chicago: Devon Avenue

Most people know it as Little India, but Devon Ave. is often called the most diverse street in America. People with ties to India, Pakistan, Bangladesh, Africa (and beyond) offer food, clothing, and items of their culture. Even the music is colorful and spicy! Landmark: Devon Gurudwara Sahib of Chicago, a Sikh temple, and Shri Swaminarayan Mandir, a Hindu temple.

Irish Chicago: Bridgeport

It's not only home to the Chicago White Sox, it's one of Chicago's oldest communities. In the 1830s, poor Irish immigrant laborers called it Hardscrabble. Now it's rich with Irish music, Irish food, and "Kiss Me, I'm Irish" T-shirts. Landmark: Nativity of Our Lord Catholic Church, one of Chicago's most historic churches.

CHICAGO for Everyone

Italian Chicago: Little Italy

This Italian community has been here since the 1880's, and it hasn't changed so much. The buildings are older, and well-kept. Longtime family grocery stores and restaurants offer traditional foods, mostly from Southern Italy. Landmark: The National Italian American Sports Hall of Fame.

Vietnamese Chicago: Little Saigon

The area may be on the small side, but this Near Southside neighborhood is the heart of Chicago's vibrant Vietnamese neighborhood. From *pho* (soup) to *banh mi* (sandwiches) to steamed buns (yum!), be sure to leave room for some unforgettable desserts you may never have heard of. Landmark: the "Asia on Argyle" sign, at the Red Line's Argyle stop.

Polish Chicago: Avondale

Did you know that Warsaw, in Poland, is the only city with more Polish people than Chicago? And in Chicago, this old-school neighborhood is still called Little Warsaw. There's more to do than eat pierogi (peer-OH-ghee) dumplings, but you'll definitely want to do that. Landmark: St. Hyacinth Basilica, a huge, ornate landmark cathedral. Event: Polish Constitution Day Parade.

Mexican Chicago: Pilsen

Just south of Downtown, you'll see walls covered in colorful murals and mosaics, celebrating the Midwest's largest Mexican community. Listen for Mariachi music, feel the original crafts, and taste a wide range of Mexican food from authentic chefs. Landmark: the National Museum of Mexican Art.

Swedish Chicago: Andersonville

The Great Fire of 1871 changed the rules about housing. Wooden houses were illegal in the city. But stone houses were expensive. To find a place where they could build wooden houses, a large group of Swedish immigrants settled together in this area north of downtown Chicago. Over the years, they built a busy community of shops, schools, and businesses, many with a Swedish touch.

What People Do

IN CHICAGO

If you lived in 19th-century Chicago, your career options were limited to things like farming, shipping, and rebuilding after big fires. Here in the 21st century, thanks to electricity, people have much better job opportunities.

Airplanes (flying): Air travel has taken off in Chicago. The country's number-three airport is O'Hare, where United Airlines' has its headquarters. American airlines has a big presence, too.

Airplanes (selling): Boeing, America's largest airline manufacturer, has its headquarters here.

More Than Airplanes: Ships and railroads are still important, while trucking, warehousing, and logistics (moving things in and out of warehouses to wherever) are also big business. Why Chicago? Because it sits on America's 50-yard line!

St. Louis may have the arch, but Chicago has the golden arches. McDonald's world headquarters drives through downtown Chicago.

What goes with McDonald's burgers? Heinz! Chicago's Kraft Heinz is America's third largest food company. If they want to grow, they have to ketchup!

Oreos? Triscuits? Ritz Crackers? You know them, but probably not the Chicago company that owns them. It's called Mondelez.

Healthcare: Between hospitals and the health industry, more than 100,000 people are taking care of Chicago when it's feeling blue. Or green.

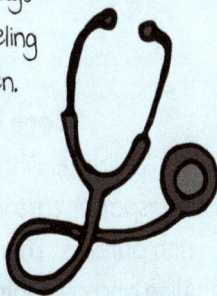

Walt Disney
Born in Chicago, December 5, 1901

Walter E. Disney failed at many early jobs—drawing newspaper cartoons, drawing ads, making baby movies for rich parents. Then he created cartoons about a girl named Alice and a rabbit named Oswald. They failed, too. Then he made a cartoon about a mouse that you've probably heard of.

Michelle Obama
Born in Chicago, January 17, 1964

Her father worked in a city factory. Her mother worked for a catalog store. After much hard work, Michelle Robinson graduated from Princeton University and Harvard Law School. At her first job, a prestigious Chicago law firm with very few Black lawyers, she met a lawyer named Barack. They married, and lived in a brick house in Chicago, until they moved to a White House in Washington.

Harrison Ford
Born in Chicago, July 13, 1942

Sometimes known as "Han" or "Indiana," Ford was the son of two Chicago actors. As a teenager he became an accomplished Boy Scout, learning skills which later helped him outrun giant rolling balls and Imperial star destroyers. Ford moved to Hollywood, spent ten years in tiny roles. Then George Lucas cast him as HanSolo in the Star Wars movies. He has also played roles as a CIA agent, the president of the United States, a Blade Runner, and a dad.

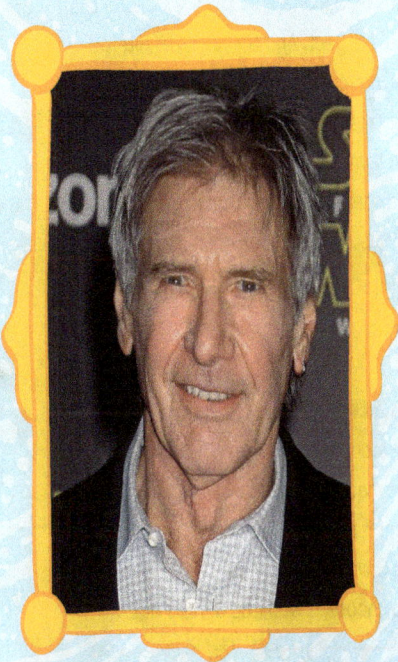

Eat the Chicago Way

Just when you think you have food figured out, along comes Chicago to turn familiar food into something completely different. And delicious!

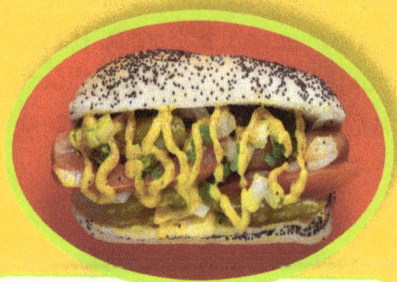

Chicago Style Hot Dog It's thicker than you'd expect. And the roll is definitely a real roll, not a squishy, thin one. Steamed, with poppy seeds. So far, so good. Then comes the tomatoes, the hot green peppers, and a kosher pickle, split the long way. A zigzag of mustard, and that's the Chicago way.

Steaks, steaks, steaks Chicago had the stockyards, where cattle once roamed. They're gone, but the best beef is still there. Everyone has a favorite Chicago steakhouse. Whichever one you choose, it won't be a mis-steak.

Jibarito If it doesn't have bread, is it a sandwich? Whatever it is, the mouth-watering Jibarito uses crunchy fried plantains (big cousins of bananas) on the ends. In between, you can get steak, pork, seafood, or even good old vegetables. Then add your hot sauce. It acts like it's from Puerto Rico, but the Jibarito is purely Chicago.

Deep Dish Pizza

Why so tall? It's what's inside that counts. These savory pies are often stuffed with pepperoni, sausage, mushrooms, peppers, onions, chunky tomatoes, and enough cheese to make three regular pizzas. The crunchy crusts are a couple inches high. And then you're stuffed, too.

Italian Beef Sandwich

This isn't your usual roast beef sammich. The beef gets simmered in a special gravy and slow cooked for most of the day. It gets sliced thin—really thin—and it's laid out on an Italian roll. What's that on top? Fried peppers. Order yours "wet" and it'll get drenched in the thin gravy. Every bite will drip watery goodness onto your pants.

Rainbow Cone

After all that meat, it's time for dessert. Original Rainbow Cone has been in business since 1926, and it's named for their star attraction. You get five flavors stacked on one cone: chocolate, strawberry, pistachio, orange sherbet, and Palmer House. That last flavor is basically cherry vanilla with walnuts, named for a fancy old Chicago hotel.

Go, Chicago Sports!

Professional sports and Chicago go way back. This city loves its teams whether they win the big trophy three years in a row, or lose for 108 years in a row.

Walter Payton

CHICAGO BEARS

Joined the National Football League in 1920.

Won the 1985 Super Bowl, and the 2006 NFC championship game. Da Bears are one of the oldest original NFL teams.

Big Names: Red Grange, Dick Butkus, Gale Sayers, Walter Payton

Home: Soldier Field

Harold Baines

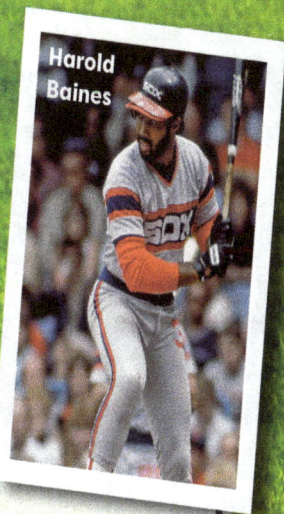

CHICAGO WHITE SOX

Joined Major League Baseball in 1900.

Won the World Series in 1906, 1917, and 2005. Their 88-year losing streak wasn't a baseball record, but it comes close. Began as the Chicago White Stockings for four years.

Big Names: Shoeless Joe Jackson, Nellie Fox, Harold Baines, Carlton Fisk, Paul Konerko

Home: Guaranteed Rate Field

CHICAGO CUBS

Joined Major League Baseball in 1876.

Won the World Series in 1907, 1908, and 2016. That's 108 years between championships, the baseball record. For this, they blamed a billy goat. Really. Until 1902, they were called the Colts or the Orphans.

Big Names: Ron Santo, Ernie Banks, Ryne Sandberg, Sammy Sosa

Home: Wrigley Field (which didn't have lights, or night games, until 1988).

WRIGLEY FIELD
HOME OF
CHICAGO CUBS
WELCOME TO
WRIGLEY FIELD

Michael Jordan

SIX-TIME NBA CHAMPIONS

CHICAGO BULLS

CHICAGO BULLS

Joined the National Basketball Association in 1966.

Won 1991-1993 championships and the 1996-1998 championships . . . the only NBA team to win two three-peats (three championships in a row).

Big Names: Michael Jordan, Scottie Pippin, Dennis Rodman, Toni Kukoc, Artis Gilmore, Chet Walker

Home: United Center

CHICAGO SKY

Joined the Women's National Basketball Association in 2006.

Played in the 2014 WNBA finals.

Big Names: Courtney Vandersloot, Allie Quigley, Elena Delle Donne

Home: Wintrust Arena

Courtney Vandersloot

CHICAGO BLACKHAWKS

Joined the National Hockey League in 1926.

Won six championship Stanley Cups, in 1934, 1938, 1961, 2010, 2013, and 2015.

The Blackhawks are one of the six original NHL teams.

Big Names: Stan Mikita, Bobby Hull, Pierre Pilote, Denis Savard, Tony Esposito

Home: United Center

CHICAGO FIRE FC

Joined Major League Soccer in 1997.

Won the MLS Championship Cup in 1998, their debut season. Also won the U.S. Open Cup in 1998 2000, 2003, and 2006.

Big Names: Piotr Nowak, Ante Razov, C.J. Brown

Home: Soldier Field

CHICAGO RED STARS

Joined Founding member of National Women's Soccer League in 2013. Was also part of two earlier pro leagues.

Played in the 2019 NWSL title game.

Big Names: Tierna Davidson, Julie Ertz

Home: SeatGeek Stadium

Other Sports!

Chicago is a great place to watch sports, but it's also a great place to DO sports. Here are some of the ways that Chicagoans like to stay active year-round.

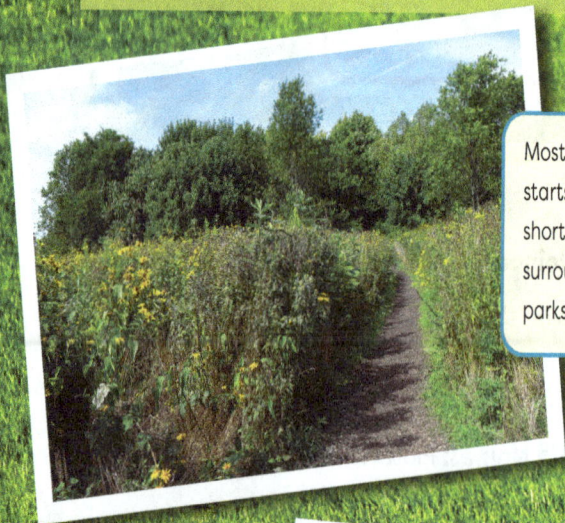

Most great **hiking** in Chicago starts with a drive or a short train ride. The city is surrounded by dozens of parks with hiking trails.

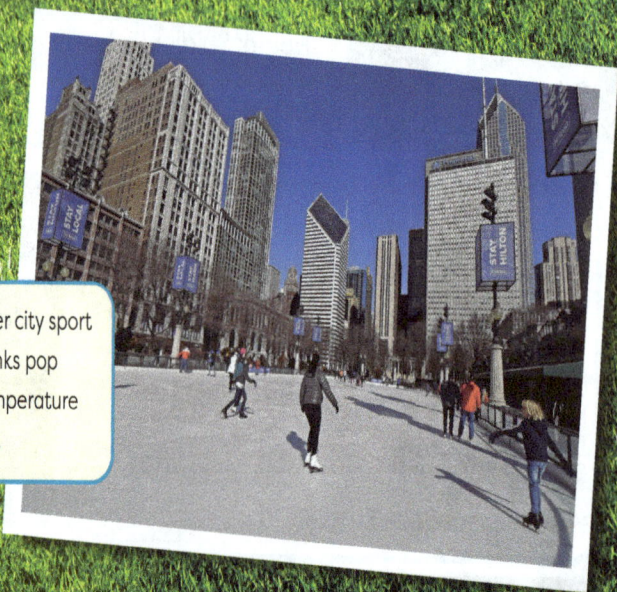

What's a better winter city sport than **ice skating**? Rinks pop up as soon as the temperature drops below freezing.

The river is not always green, but no matter what color, it's a great place to **kayak** in spring and summer.

Lakefront Park has an 18-mile **bicycle** trail, but that's just part of the city's 200 miles of bike lanes and routes.

The Lakefront Trail is also the city's best **running** route, but it's just one of many scenic places to jog.

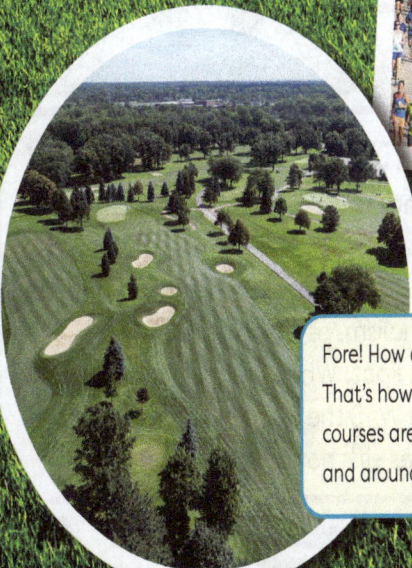

Fore! How about 200? That's how many **golf** courses are located in and around Chicago.

COLLEGE TOWN

Chicago and the cities nearby are home to several very important colleges.

UNIVERSITY OF CHICAGO

Founded 1890
Students: 7,000
Popular majors: Social sciences, math/stats, biology
Fast Fact: Students and staff take part each year in "Scav," a three-day treasure hunt around Chicago.

THE UNIVERSITY OF **CHICAGO**

NORTHWESTERN UNIVERSITY

Founded 1851
Students: 8,400
Popular majors: economics, journalism, psychology
Fast Fact: When it was founded, this area WAS the Northwest of the United States—it's not any more!

Northwestern University

UNIVERSITY OF ILLINOIS–CHICAGO

Founded 1859
Students: 20,000
Popular majors: health sciences
Fast Fact: Part of a statewide group, UIC was formed by connecting several health- and medicine-related schools.

LOYOLA UNIVERSITY

Founded 1870
Students: 12,000
Popular majors: biology, nursing, psychology
Fast Fact: A Catholic school run by the Jesuits, it's one of six different Loyola Universities in the U.S.

DEPAUL UNIVERSITY

Founded 1898
Students: 14,000
Popular majors: business, communications, performing arts
Fast Fact: Founded by a group of priests called Vincentians, it's the largest Catholic University in the U.S.

LOL!

Laugh with Chi-town!

Go ahead and laugh at Chicago—its people won't mind! Here are some riddles to tickle your funny bone.

What do you call a loud person in Chicago?

Illi*noisy*!

Which stadium can't stay still?

Wriggly Field!

What's the hardest field in Chicago?

The Field Museum—it's made of stone!

What's Queen Elizabeth's favorite fountain?

Buckingham Fountain!

What's long and green and soaking wet?

The Chicago River on St. Patrick's Day!

What's the world's tallest vegetable?

The Bean!

What is Han Solo's favorite place in Chicago?

Millenium Park!

Why do Chicago TVs use the biggest satellite dishes?

Because deep dish is the best!

Why can't you believe what the statues at the entrance to the Art Institute say?

They're both *lyin'*!

It's Alive! Animals in Chicago

Chicago's a big city with a lot of nature nearby. . . and that means lots of places for animals to live. You can find them in all sorts of open spaces, on land and sea. And some of them don't mind visiting people at home. If you think Chicago is going to the birds, you might be right. They're spotting new species all the time!

Downy woodpecker

Black-crowned night heron

Eastern cottontail rabbit

Merganser

Nighthawk

Opossum

WE SAW IT AT THE ZOO

What started with two swans, now has more than 1,100 animals . . . and is always free? Chicago's awesome Lincoln Park Zoo! In 1868, Chicago got a pair of swans from New York City as a gift. The birds were the start of what became the Lincoln Park Zoo, one of America's biggest and best wildlife homes. More than three million people visit the zoo each year, one of the city's biggest tourist sites.

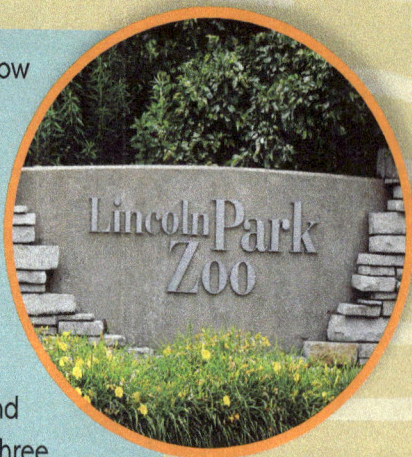

At the Farm-in-the-Zoo, meet and pet barnyard animals. Ride a train, see apes and monkeys, check out the children's zoo, and much more. The McCormick Bird House opened in 1904!

Lions

Macaques

Seals

Bald eagle

Great apes

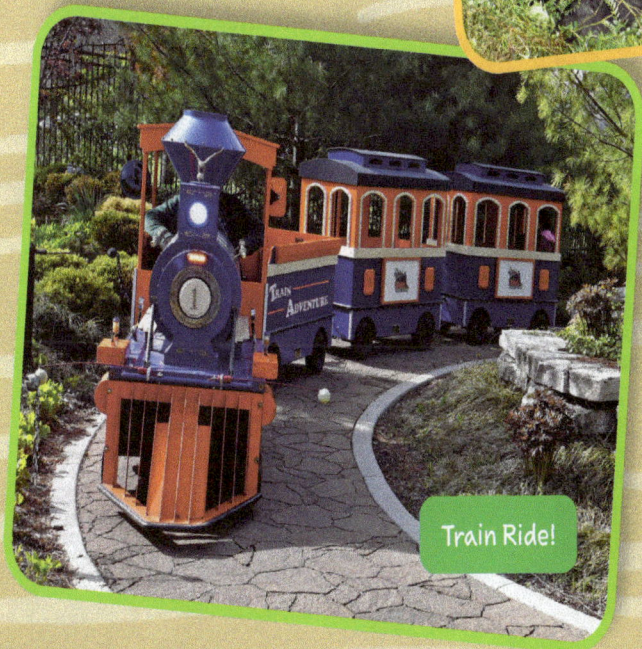
Train Ride!

CHICAGO BY THE NUMBERS

Stats and facts and digits galore: Here are some of the numbers that make Chicago what it is.

Start Here!

The famous road that ends in California starts in Chicago.

HISTORIC
ILLINOIS
U S
66
ROUTE

BEGIN

NO. 2, PART 1

With more than 1.5 million daily riders, the Chicago subway is the second-largest in the country (behind New York City).

NO. 2, PART 2

Wrigley Field is the second-oldest ballpark in the Major Leagues (behind Boston's Fenway Park).

16"

The size around the ball used in a form of softball popular all over Chicago . . . but almost nowhere else!

The first Ferris wheel spun around at the 1893 Exposition. It was invented by, you guessed, a guy named George Washington Ferris.

26

Miles of

Lake Michigan

beachfront

within city limits.

The first-ever organized car race in America was held in Chicago in 1895.

The first all-color TV station opened in 1956.

Spooky Sights

Do ghosts live in Chicago? Do spirits haunt the buildings? Whether you believe in stuff like this or not, there are many haunting tales told in the Windy City!

Congress Plaza Hotel

If you worry about ghosts, you might not sleep well at this hotel. Guests and workers have said they spotted several spirits. "Peg Leg Johnny" was killed at the hotel and some think he has stuck around! One room in particular is said to be home to various shades and apparitions. Hope you don't get that one!

Drake Hotel

A woman dressed in a red dress is said to have haunted this hotel near the lake since the 1920s. She has been spotted in some of the hotel's fancy dining rooms—maybe she's just hungry!

Red Lion Pub

Anyone trying to enjoy a night out at this bar should be ready for anything! Ghost sightings have included a spooky man with a beard, a cowboy, and a woman in a 1920s flapper dress!

The Water Tower

This famous Chicago building survived the Great Fire (page 18), but a worker who was in the building at the time did not. He was very brave, however, staying behind to make sure water could get out to firefighters. Visitors say his spirit is still around, working the pumps!

Graceland Cemetery

A haunted cemetery is nothing new, right? But this one has a statue of a young girl that disappears in the rain! Her parents put it up when she died after being struck by lightning. Workers say that during heavy rain, the statue vanishes! Is the girl back . . . or not?

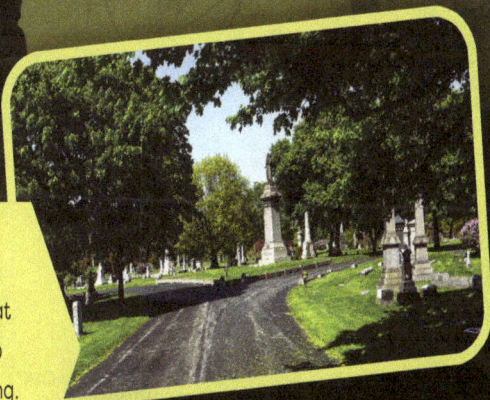

One Big Lake!

Lake Michigan

While Chicago is a busy city, packed with buildings, roads, parks, and people, it's right next to something even bigger—Lake Michigan. You can't ignore this massive body of water, no matter where you are in the city. Here are some amazing facts about Chicago's watery neighbor.

Map labels: Lake Superior, CANADA, MICHIGAN, Straits of Mackinac, Lake Huron, WISCONSIN, Lake Michigan, MICHIGAN, ILLINOIS, Chicago, INDIANA, OHIO

Petoskey stone is a type of coral. It's found only on the shore of this lake.

LAKE MICHIGAN FAST FACTS

• Third largest of the Great Lakes.

• Touches four states: Michigan (of course!), Indiana, Illinois, and Wisconsin

• Average depth: 279 feet

• Maximum depth: 925 feet

• Only Great Lake that is entirely inside the United States. The other four are each partly in Canada.

So many ships sank at the **Straits of Mackinac** that it's now an underwater museum that divers can visit.

It's Alive! Lake Michigan Animals

The enormous lake isn't home to any people, but it sure has a lot of animal life! Whether it swims, flies, walks, or crawls, animals of all sorts depend on the enormous lake for shelter and food. Keep an eye out for these cool critters when you walk on the shore or sail on the water!

Largemouth bass

Swans

Freshwater sponge

Hawks

Sea lamprey

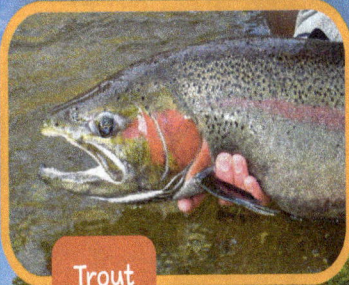
Trout

Tons o' Ducks

Here are some of the species of ducks that live on or near Lake Michigan:

American Black Duck
Black scoter
Blue-winged teal
Buffleheads
Long-tailed
Mallard
Merganser (right)
Pintail

FAST FACT
Scientists divide ducks into two types: divers, which go underwater to snag food; dabblers, who mostly eat plants they can reach on the surface.

Not Far Away

Whether you live in Chicago or you're just visiting the city, don't forget that many other awesome places to visit are very close by. Get a driver and hit the road for these fun day (or so!) trips.

We just got back to our hotel after visiting **The Forge**. And I am wiped out!

Why are you so tired?

You won't believe all the things we did at The Forge! It's an adventure park about an hour west of Chicago. They have so much to do there, it would take days to do it all.

Like what?

Zip line . . . laser tag . . . mountain biking . . . canoeing . . . climbing walls . . .

Slow down! You're making ME tired.

It's in an area called the **Lemont Quarries**. Along with the Forge, there are beautiful parks and lakes to explore.

What are quarries?

I read that they are old places where people did mining.

Sounds like you didn't "mind" a lot of fun!

Want to see amazing plants? Head north out of Chicago to a small town called Glencoe.

What's there?

The **Chicago Botanic Garden**! They have thousands of amazing plants to check out.

What was your favorite?

Not sure I can pick just one. I loved the big fields of color, though!

Awesome! I'll get out my hiking shoes!

It's not just flowers, either. There are lots of hikes and long walks alongside beautiful lakes and ponds.

Splish, splash!

Just for walking . . . not for swimming!

Did you know you can go to Africa about two hours northwest of Chicago?

Well, I know I'm no geography whiz, but that sounds impossible!

Well, it's true . . . sort of. We visited **Safari Lake Geneva**. That's in Wisconsin. And it was, I guess, sort of like a real safari! For one thing, these giant-horned Watusi cows only live in Africa!

Cool! What else did you see?

Camels, zebras, yaks, and lots more.

Hope you didn't try to ride any of them!

Ha! No way! It's a car safari. You ride in your own car through this huge grassy area.

Nice!

Yeah. The animals sometimes come right near your car.

What else did you see?

Well, I'd never seen one of these before. It's called an Addax!

After all that animal excitement, we needed something quiet. We found it at **Waterfall Glen Preserve**.

I once knew a guy named Glen Davis. Any relation?

Ha. No! This is a beautiful park with miles and miles of hiking trails. It's centered on this beautiful waterfall and river.

Wow, that does look relaxing!

We took a picnic lunch and wandered to the falls. There were tons of birds and we even saw some cool salamanders like this guy!

Creepy! Cool, but a little creepy!

Ah, you're such a worrier. He was fine! I gotta go . . . we're heading off to another adventure. Next stop: Europe!

Wait . . . what?

Holland, Michigan

How can you make a trip to a country in Europe . . . that is not far from Chicago? Head across the lake to Holland! The city was founded in 1847 by immigrants from the Netherlands (Holland is a region of that country). It has become a Dutch-themed village popular with tourists from all over the country.

We were here for Tulip Time! The event started in 1927. Every year, people come to see the thousands of tulips that are opening up in the spring.

In 1964, the town bought a real windmill from Holland . . . the one in Europe! It's called the DeZwaan windmill, and is the only one in the United States! It's on (naturally) Windmill Island, surrounded by acres of tulips!

We rang bells, saw how wooden shoes are made, and watched Dutch dancers at Nelis' Dutch Village.

Head to the lake! Or should I say "lakes"? Holland has shores on Lake Michigan and Lake Macatawa. Both have long beaches, lakeside parks, and hiking trails to explore.

Sister Cities Around the World

Cities have sisters? That's right! Inspired by a national program started in the 1950s, cities big and small across America team up with cities around the world. They become Sister Cities. (Why not Brother Cities? Sister Cities sounds better—alliteration . . . look it up!) As one of America's biggest cities, Chicago has one of the biggest Sister City programs, with 30 Sisters . . . and counting!

Plus these Sisters!
Mexico City, Mexico
Milan, Italy
Moscow, Russia
Paris, France
Petach Tikva, Israel
Prague, Czech Republic
Shanghai, China
Shenyang, China
Vilnius, Lithuania
Warsaw, Poland

Gothenburg, Sweden
Galway, Ireland
Hamburg, Germany
Birmingham, United Kingdom
Kyiv, Ukraine
Lucerne, Switzerland
Belgrade, Serbia
Toronto, Canada
Athens, Greece
Osaka, Japan
Casablanca, Morocco
Amman, Jordan
Lahore, Pakistan
Busan, Republic of Korea
Delhi, India
Bogotá, Colombia
Accra, Ghana
Durban, South Africa
Sydney, Australia

Chicago's Sister Cities

Sister Cities in Action

Here are some examples of how Chicago is working with and helping its sister cities:

Chicago welcomes young women from Sister Cities around the world to its annual Global Youth Ambassador program. Dozens of teens connect in person or virtually to share their stories, learn about each other's lives and cultures, and learn how to be leaders in their home countries.

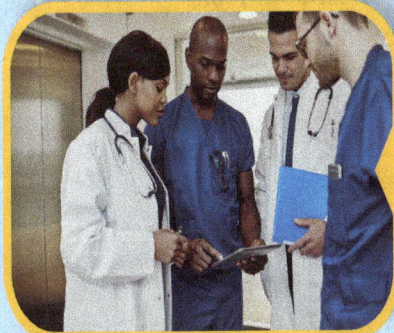

Another Chicago program connects doctors fighting cancer. Doctors from Sister Cities like Accra, Lahore, and Osaka come to Chicago to learn more. They are able to take home new techniques to fight disease.

The COVID-19 crisis showed how important it is for people around the world to communicate. Chicago and its Sister City of Shanghai had several virtual events to share information. One helped caregivers in each country learn new ways to help seniors who were battling COVID and other illnesses.

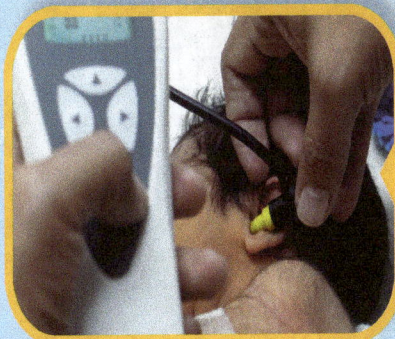

Chicago helps its Sister Cities. Recent donations have included money to help buy hearing aids for children in Bogotá, Colombia, and Amman, Jordan. The money also helped with hearing testing for young children.

Books, Websites, and More!

Books

Coleman, Ted. *Chicago Bears: All-Time Greats.* North Star Books, 2020.

Currie, Lindsay. *Scritch Scratch.* Sourcebooks Young Readers, 2018. (Note: a spooky ghost novel!)

Guendeslberger, Erin. *Hide and Seek Chicago.* Sourcebooks Wonderland, 2019.

Magsamen, Sarah. *ABCs of Chicago.* Hometown World, 2021.

Pascal, Jane. *What Was the Great Chicago Fire?* Penguin Workshop, 2016.

Whiting, Jim. *Chicago Cubs.* Creative Paperbacks, 2020.

Web Sites

https://www.choosechicago.com/articles/
families/30-kid-friendly-things-to-do-
in-chicago/
The city tourism experts made this list of
things to do in Chicago.

https://www.chicagokids.com/
A great place for parents and families to find
kid-friendly activites in Chicagoland.

Photo Credits and Thanks

Photos from Dreamstime, Library of Congress, Shutterstock,
or Wikimedia unless otherwise noted. 22: Everett Collection/Alamy
Stock Photo. 67: David Batel/ISI/Zuma/Newscom.

Artwork: LemonadePixel. Maps: Jessica Nevins (6-7).

Cultural Content Consultant: Jennifer E. Ellwood.

Thanks to our pal Nancy Ellwood and the fine folks at Arcadia!

INDEX

Thanks for Visiting

CHICAGO

Come Back Soon!